NATIONAL GEOGRAPHIC

Families

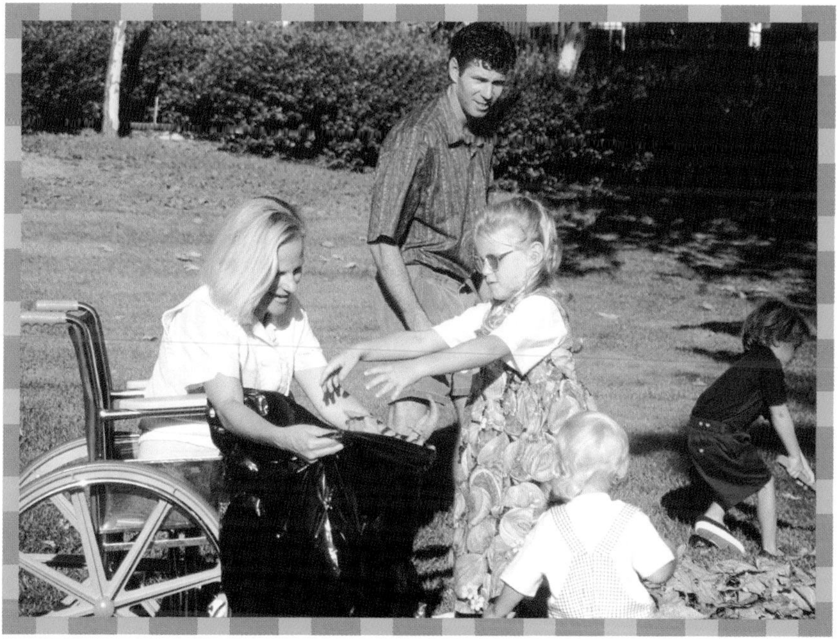

Rose Lorenzo

T0308249

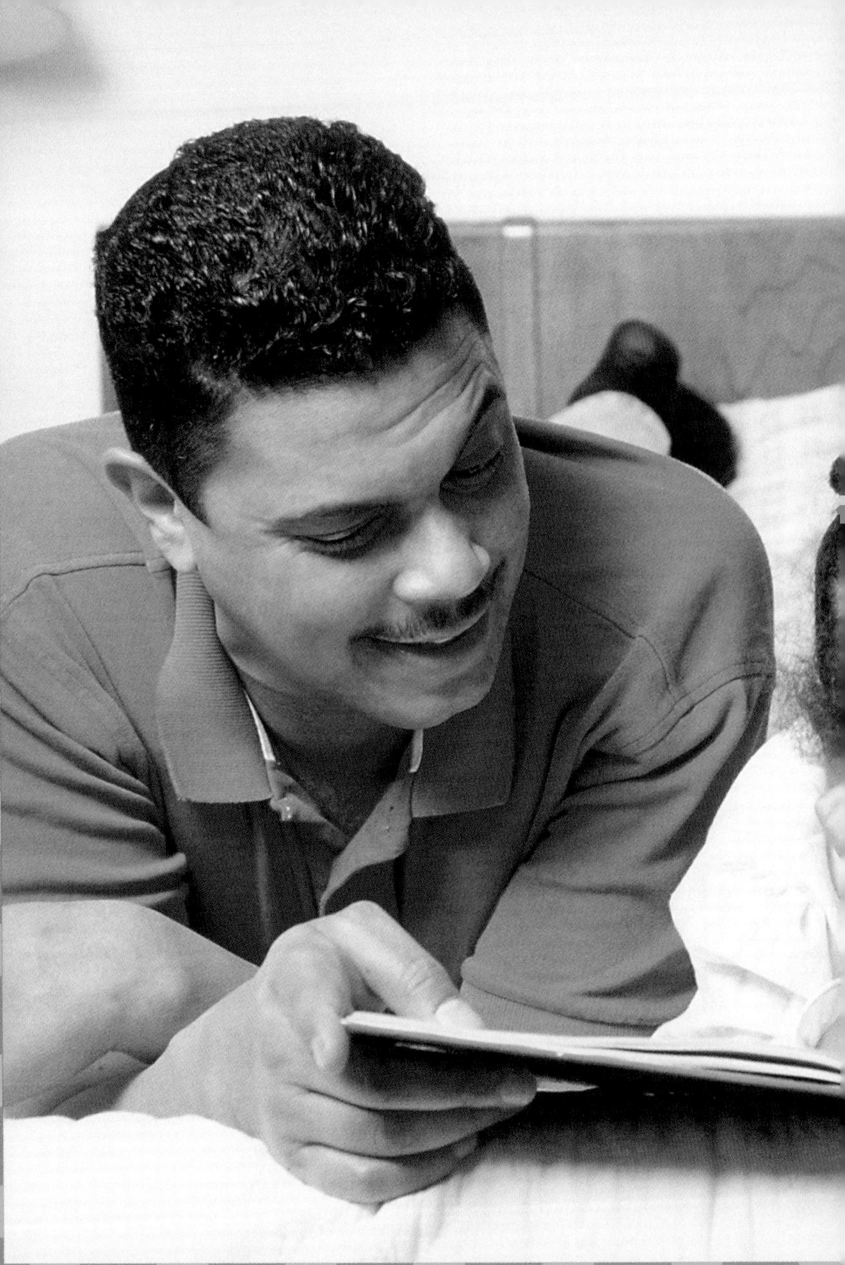

read

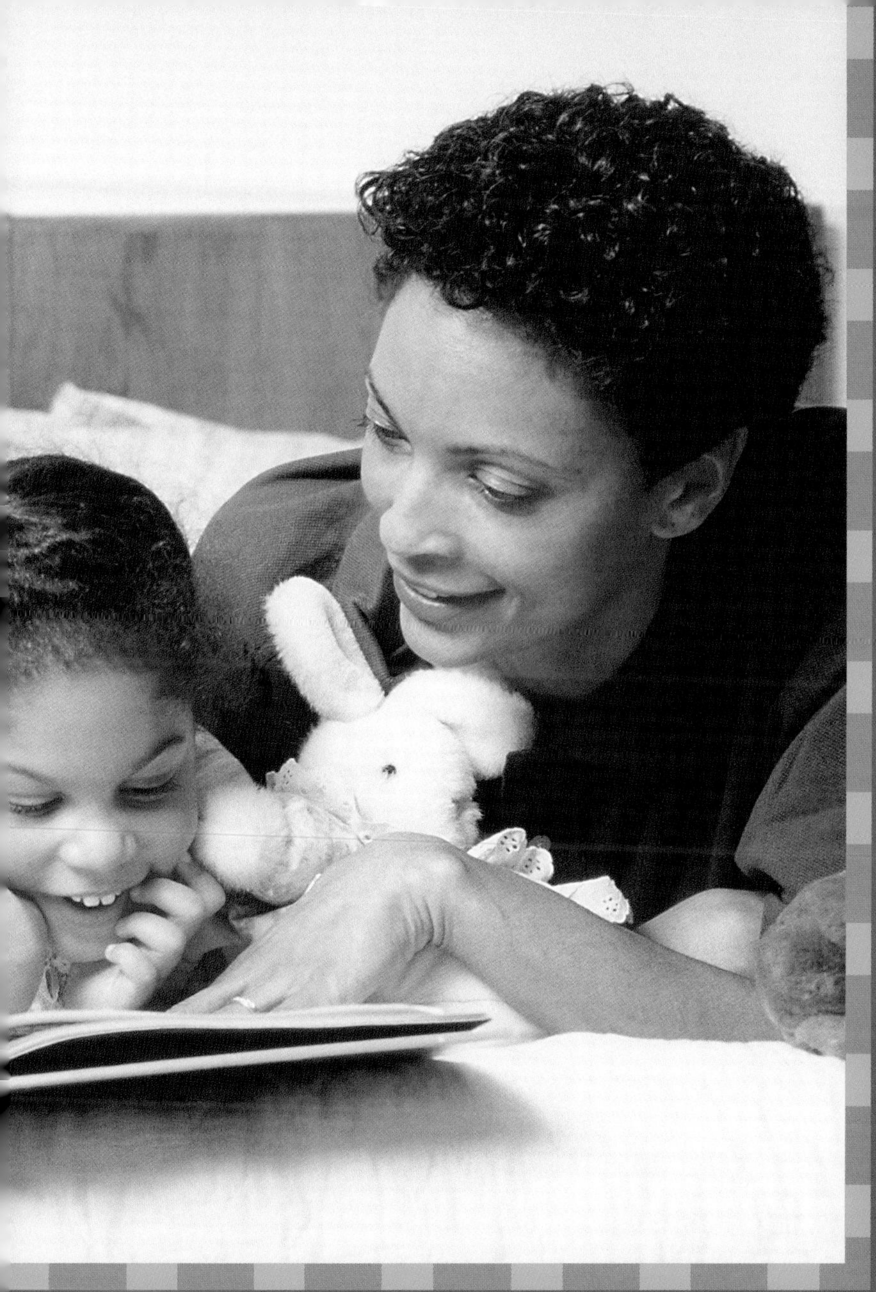

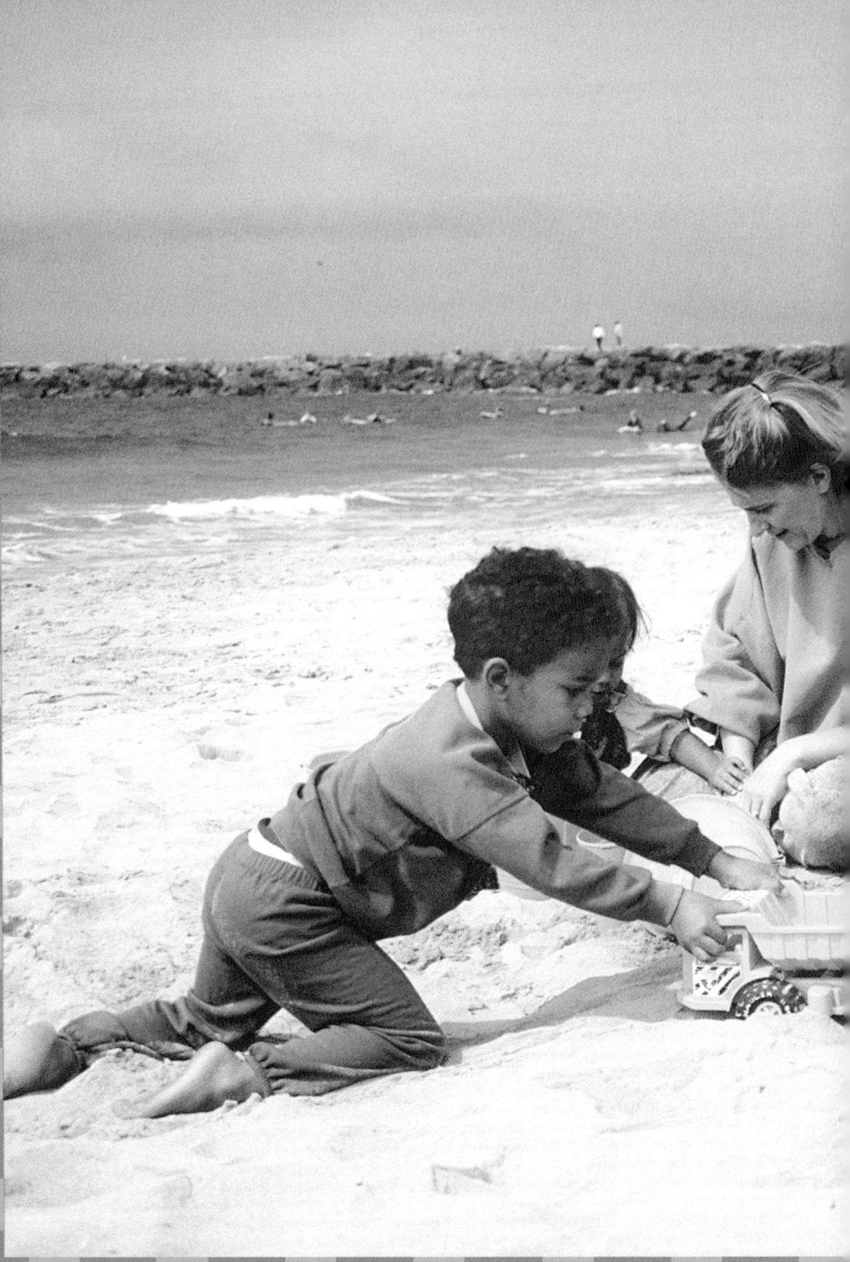

play

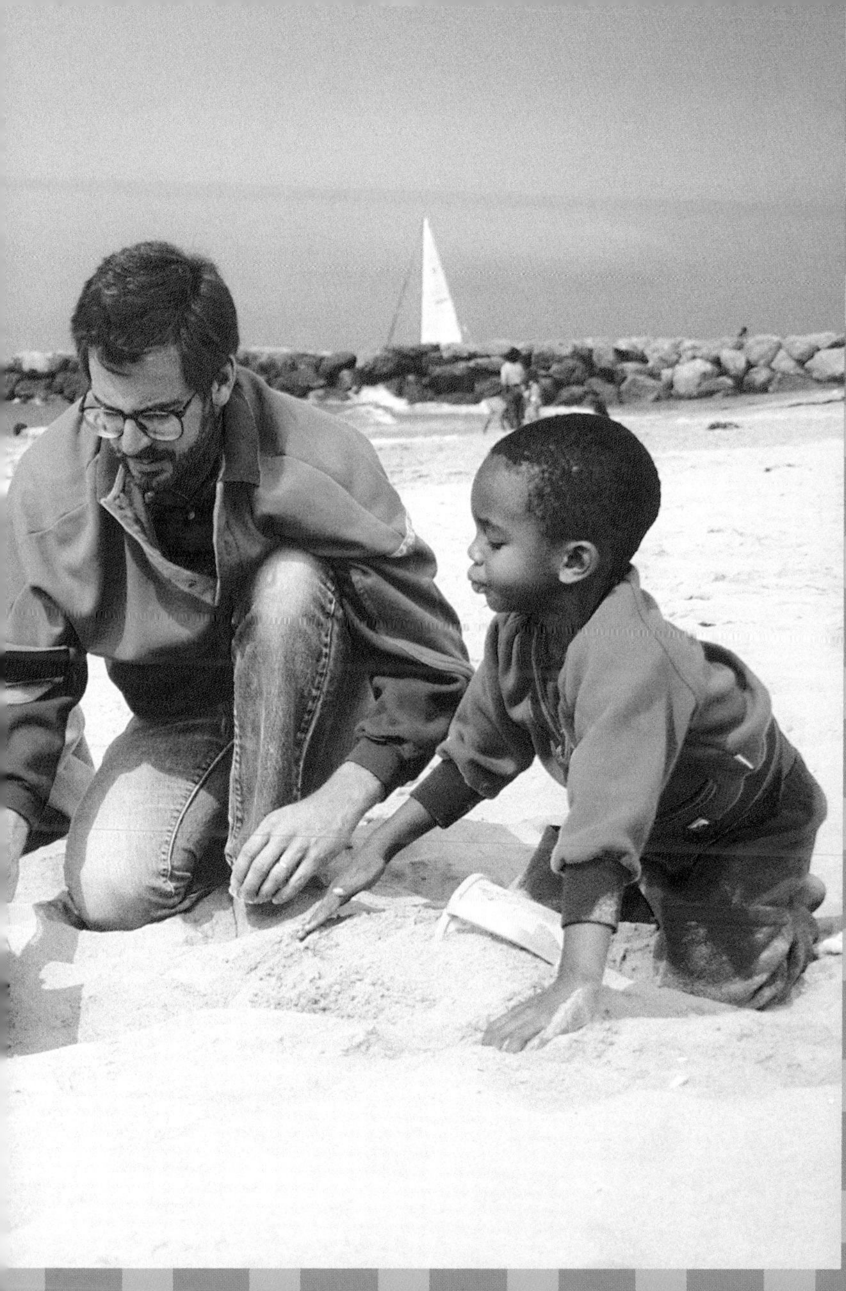

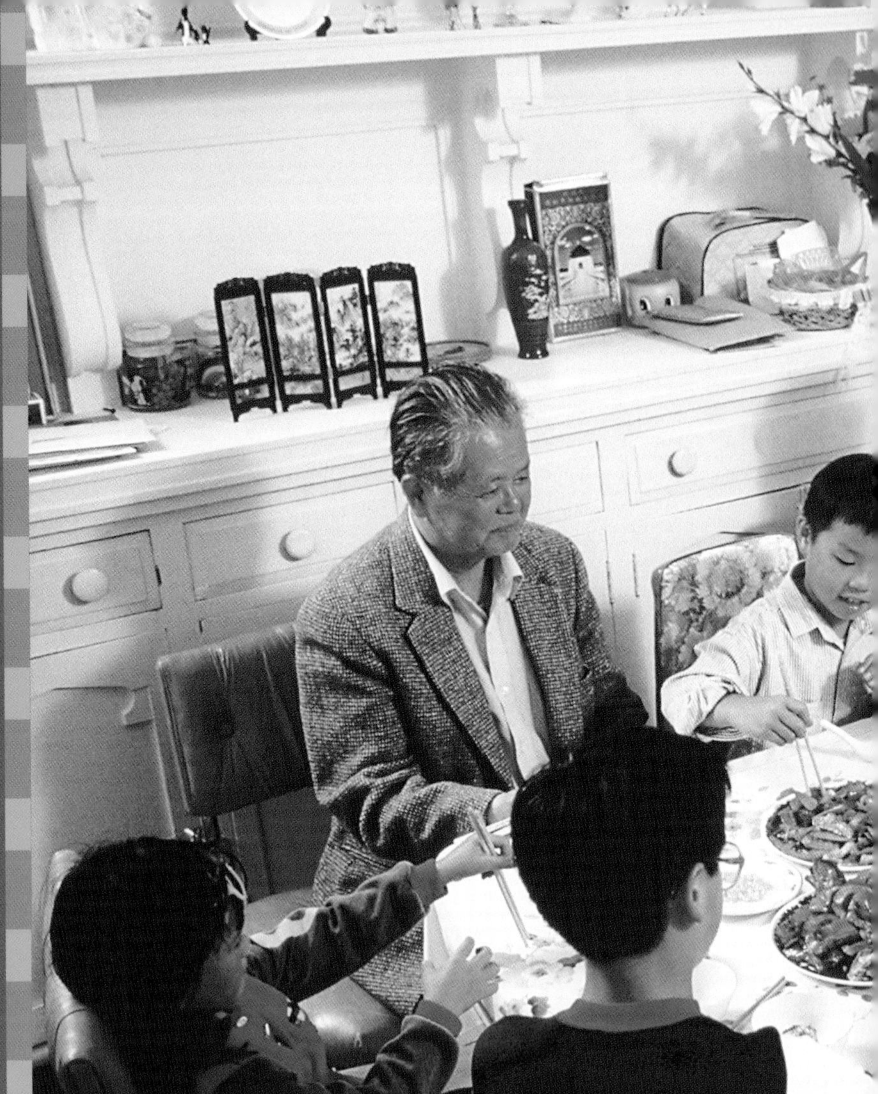

eat

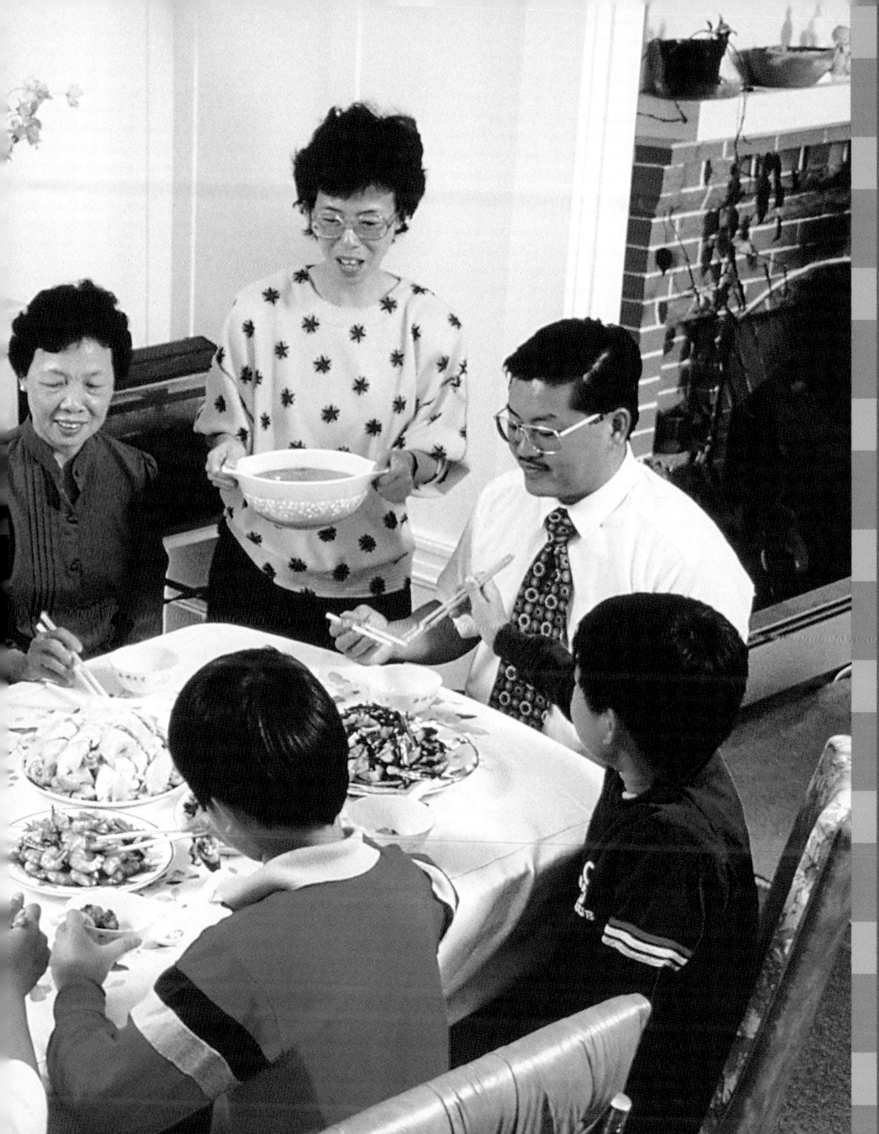

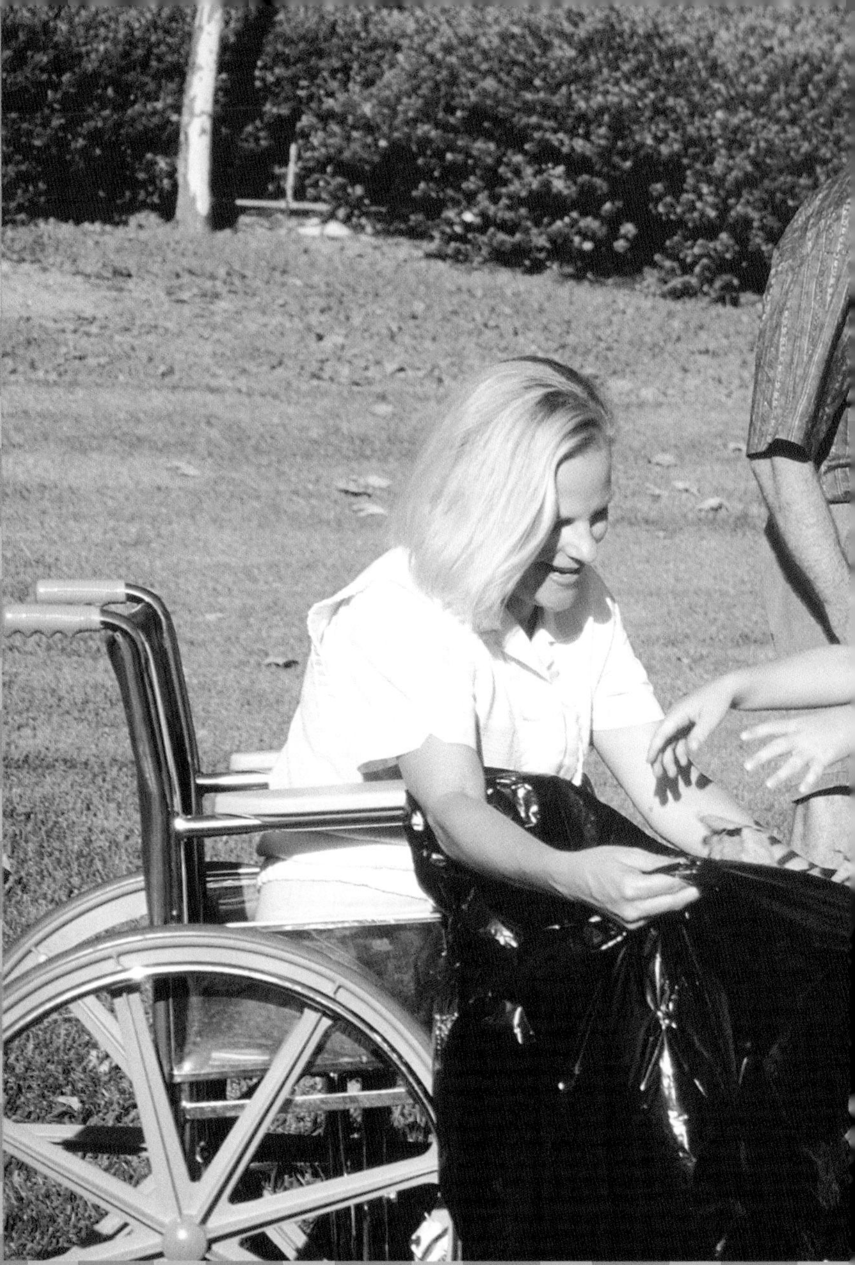

work

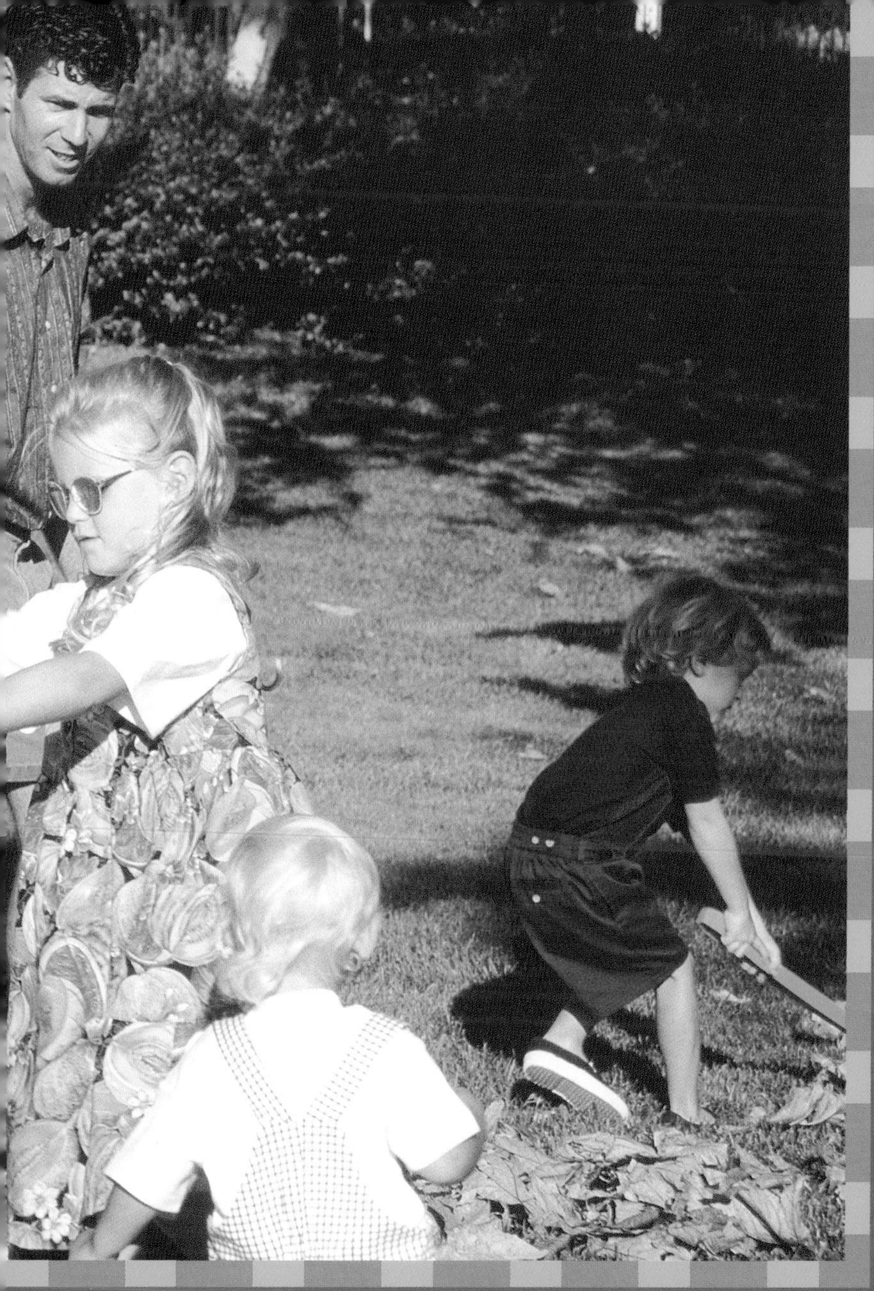

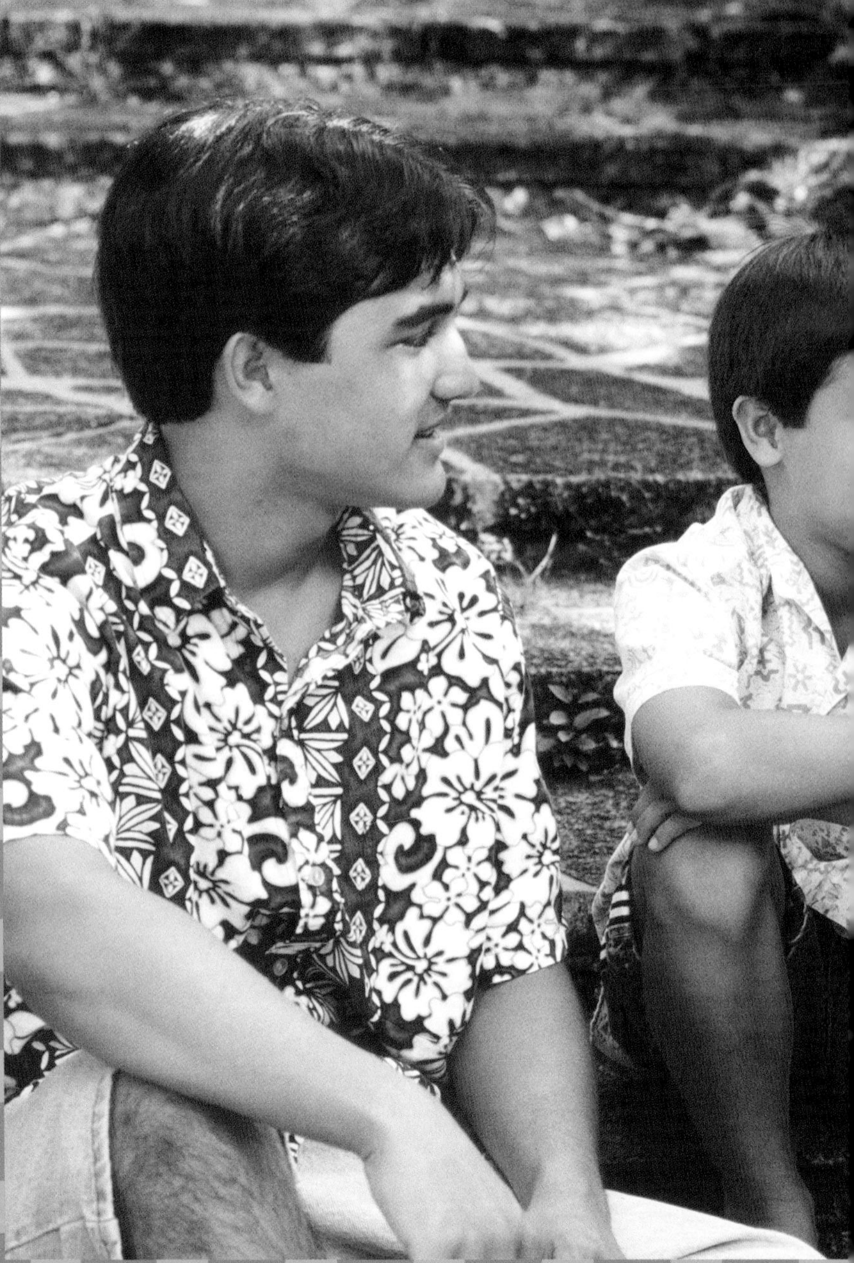

talk

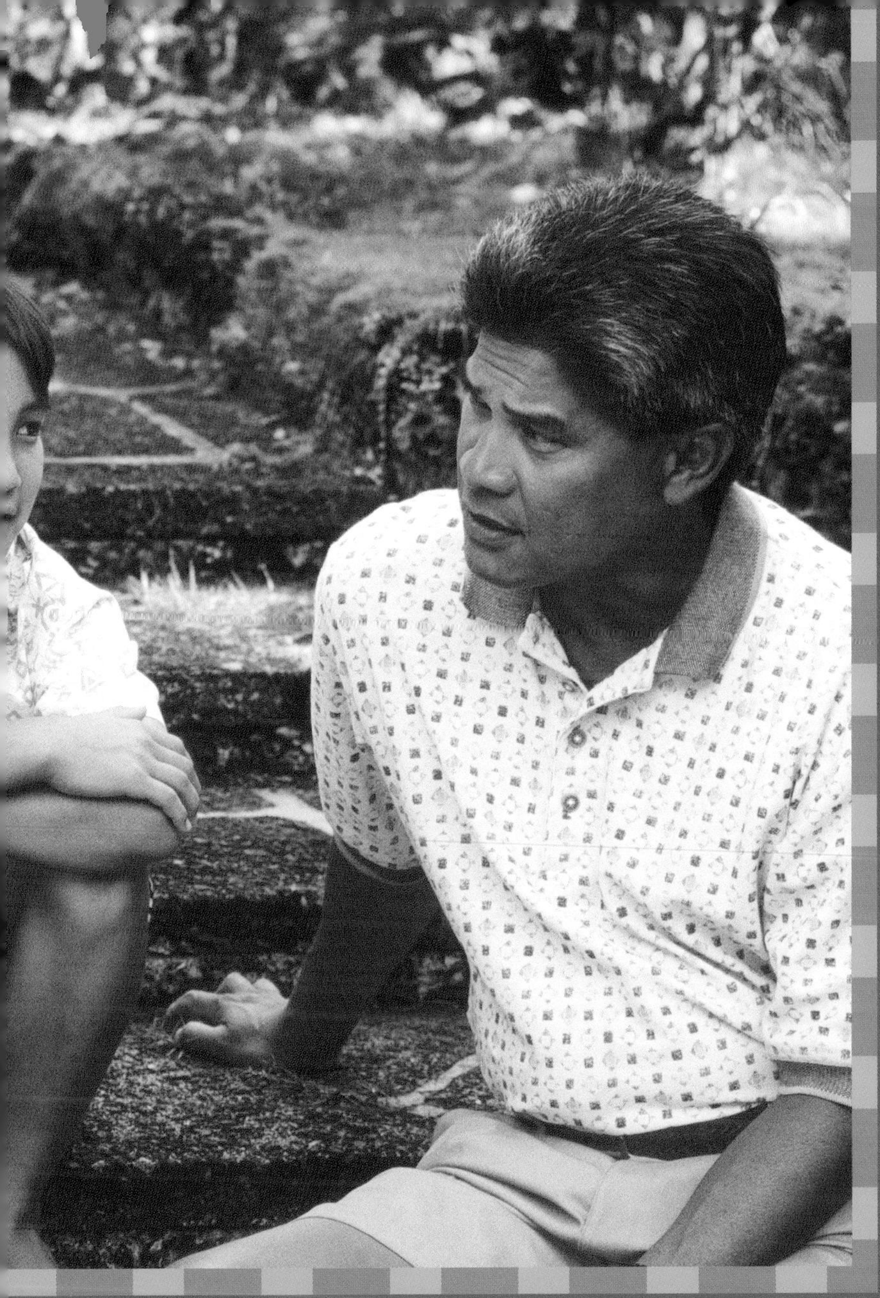

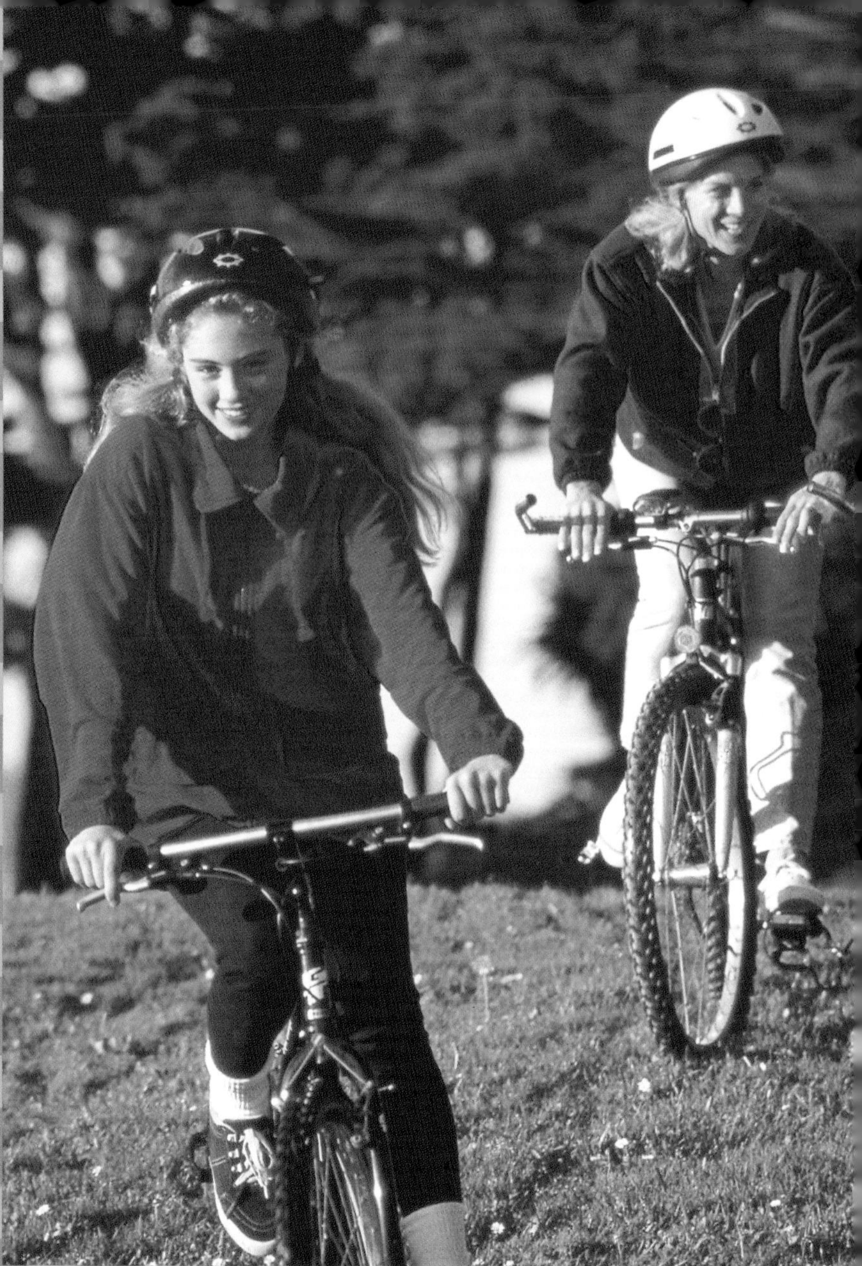

ride

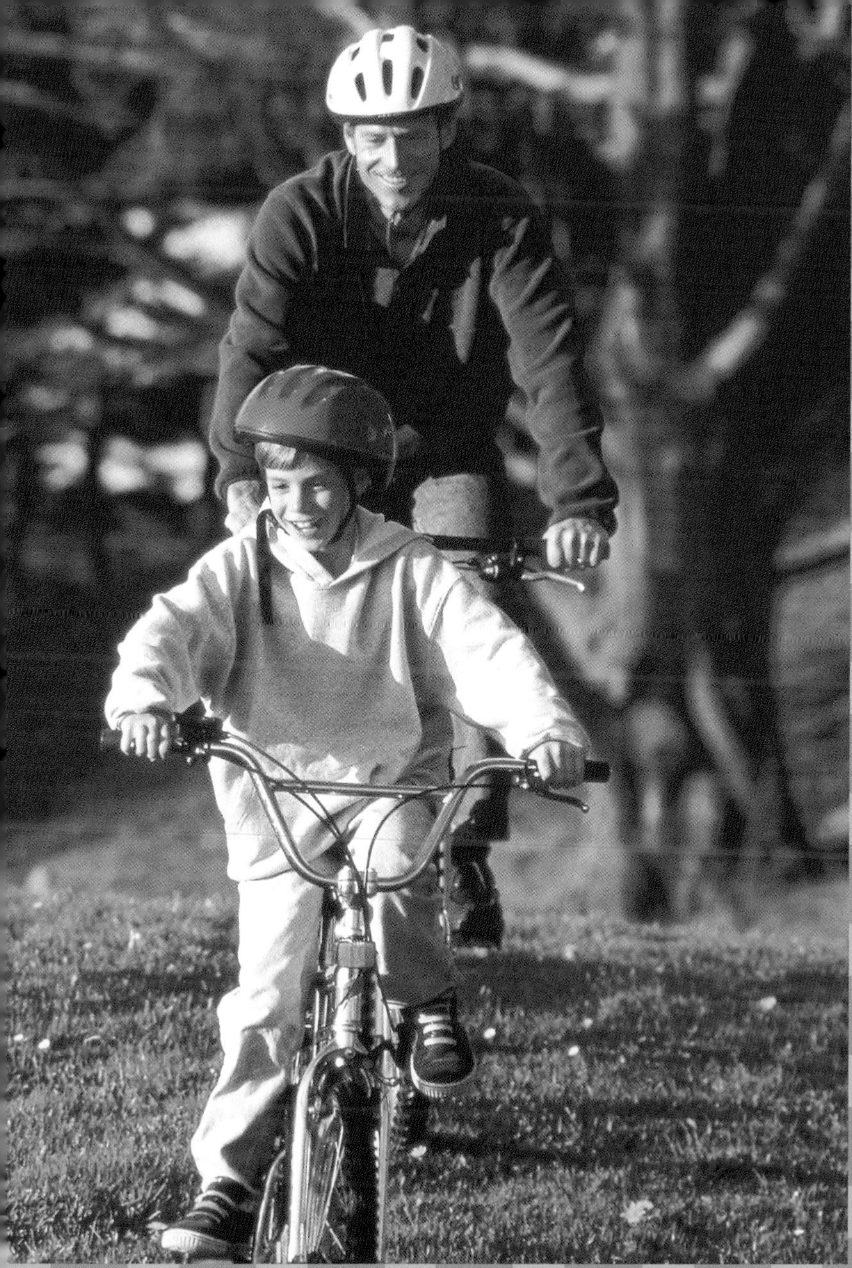

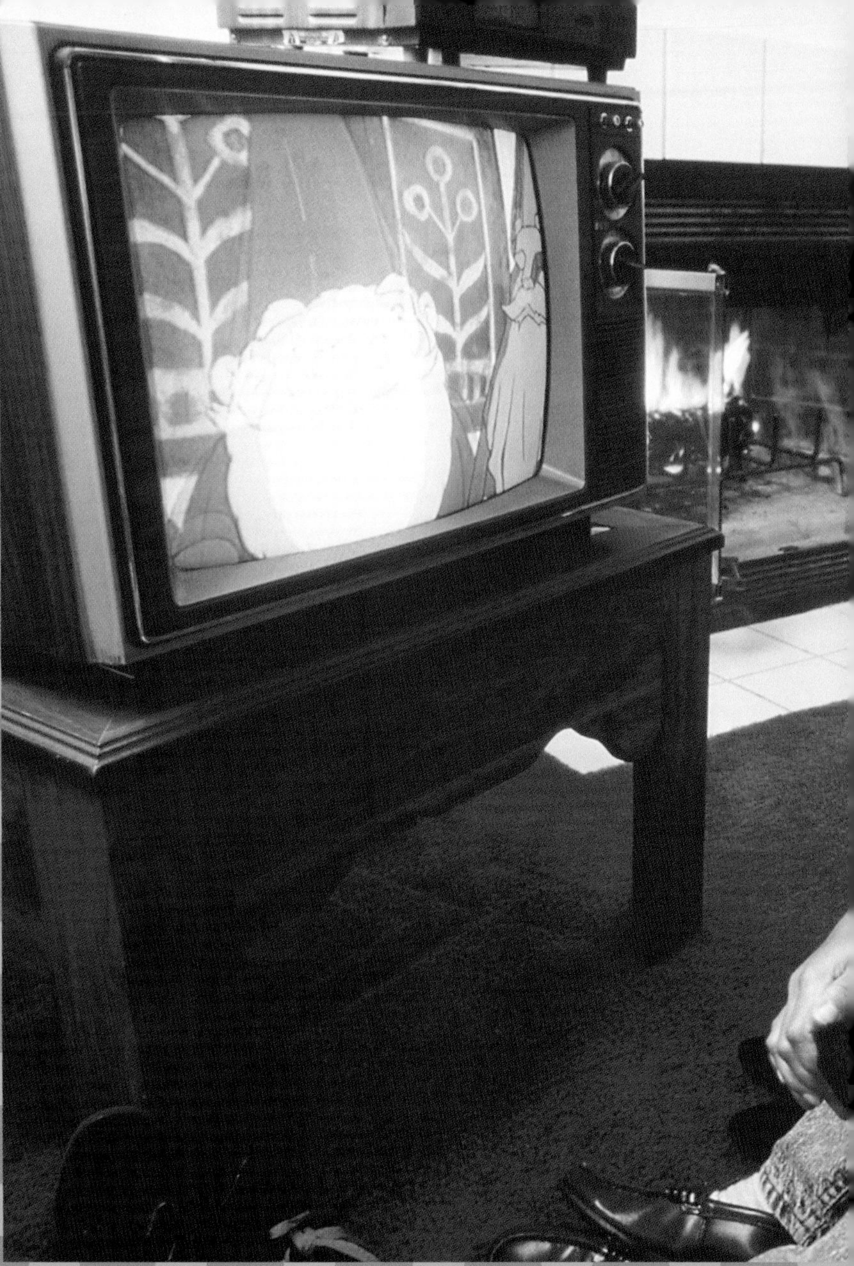

watch

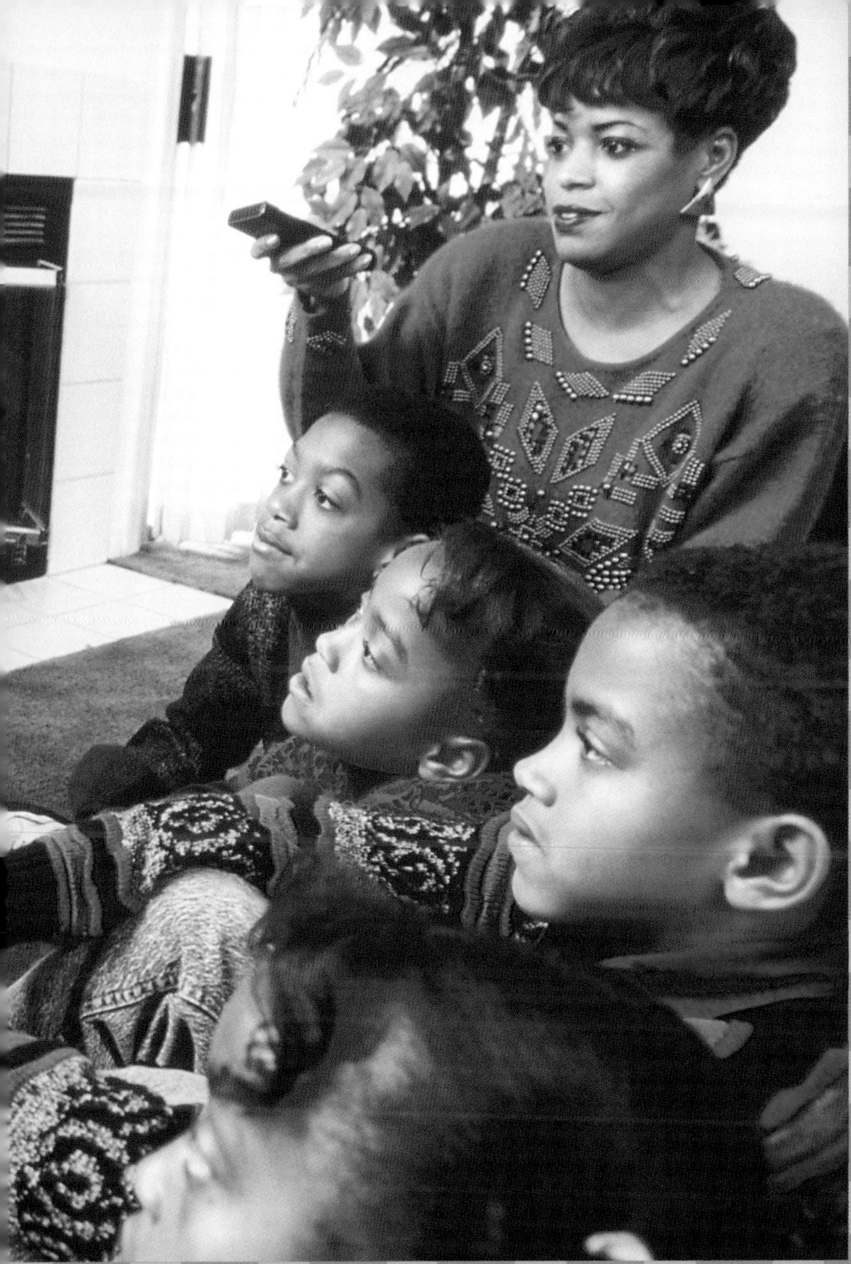

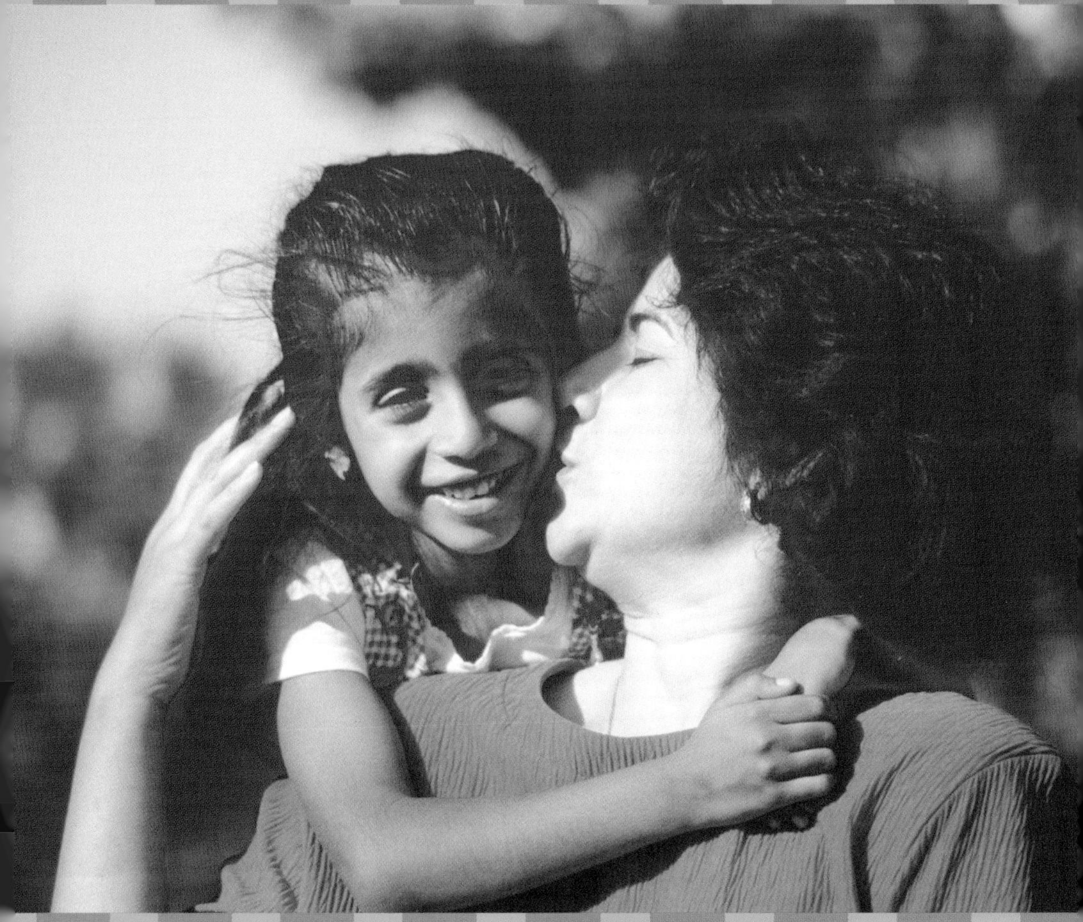

hug